Adventure Boys!

ADVENTURE BOYS!

Crafts and Activities for Curious, Creative, Courageous Boys

NICOLE DUGGAN

ILLUSTRATED BY CAIT BRENNAN

R

**ROCKRIDGE
PRESS**

Interior and Cover Designer: Tricia Jang
Art Producer: Tom Hood
Editor: Laura Apperson
Production Editor: Ashley Polikoff

Illustrations © Cait Brennan 2021

ISBN: Print 978-1-64876-214-7 | eBook 978-1-64876-215-4

R0

To my children,
Blake and Natalie,
who are my favorite people
to go on adventures with.

CONTENTS

INTRODUCTION

I wrote this book for you, Adventure Boy, to inspire you to try new things and share your talents with the world.

In this book you will discover information about coding, training your pets, and taking care of the planet. You will be introduced to different art techniques, how to make your own documentary, how to entertain with magic tricks, and so much more! My goal is for you to find something that fascinates you that you want to continue to learn more about.

There are extraordinary people featured in this book who changed the world because they showed the courage to follow their passions and challenged themselves to achieve their goals. I hope their stories inspire you to follow your dreams and not give up.

My hope is that this book will encourage you to explore something new, help the world around you, and to spread kindness as you go.

BE ADVENTUROUS, BE BRAVE, BE CREATIVE, AND—MOST IMPORTANT—BE YOU!

Around the Block

Your neighborhood includes the people, animals, plants, and buildings around where you live. Adventure Boys enjoy discovering what makes their neighborhood and community interesting and unique.

NEIGHBORHOOD BINGO

Turn a walk in your neighborhood into a fun game of bingo! Ask your siblings or friends to join you and test your observation skills.

WHAT YOU'LL NEED

☐ Paper or card stock
☐ Pencil

1. Work together to brainstorm a list of 24 items that you think you will come across as you explore your neighborhood. Think of things such as an insect, a red mailbox, a bird's nest, a fire hydrant, a circle-shaped window, or a building with a certain colored door.

2. Draw a grid of 25 squares on a piece of paper by making five rows of five squares.

3. Make a FREE space in the middle square of the third row by writing FREE or coloring it in.

4. Next, all players should fill in the other squares by writing the items from the list onto their card. Put them in a random order so that everyone's card is different.

5. As a group, walk through the neighborhood to hunt for things listed on your card.

6. When someone finds an item, announce it. Each player can cross it off on their own bingo card.

7. The first player to get five in a row (up to down, side to side, or diagonal) wins!

MAKE YOUR OWN MAP

Maps are helpful for getting to know an area, finding your way, or planning a space. Adventure Boys can pay attention to detail to make their own maps.

WHAT YOU'LL NEED

☐ Paper
☐ Markers or crayons

LEGEND

- - - Road   ⠿ Fire Station
≈ River   ⟫ Police Station
○ Lake   ▦ School
△▲△ Park   † Church
☐ Library   △ Museum

1. Decide what you want to draw a map of. Choose a place that you are familiar with, such as your neighborhood, school, or park.

2. Draw an outline of your space. Look closely at the edges of the area you are drawing to make it the same shape. Your map won't always be a square.

3. Before you begin to draw the details of your space, you will want to add a legend. A legend is a chart with symbols that represent different things. For example, blue lines for rivers, squares for houses, circles for bushes, and ovals for trees. The symbols in the legend make it easier to draw and read a map.

4. Draw the details of your space, starting with the biggest items. Make sure to add symbols to your legend.

5. Pay attention to how close or far apart things are in your space. Are they spread out or next to each other? Does your map match?

DRAW YOUR NEIGHBORHOOD

Now that you've explored your neighborhood, have fun drawing a picture of something you found interesting.

Your Neighborhood in the Day

During the day, you can see all of the colors and shadows that the sun creates. Draw a picture of something in your neighborhood. Pay attention to different details. You could draw a sign that caught your attention, a uniquely shaped tree, or a place that you like to visit.

Your Neighborhood in the Evening

As the sun sets, the sky glows with different colors, while buildings, trees, and cars become darker. Use a black crayon or marker to draw a landmark, like a building or tree that you've seen in your neighborhood. Then use lighter colors such as yellow, orange, red, and pink to shade in the sky. Put the darkest sky color at the top of the paper and keep adding lighter colors as you work your way down.

MAKE YOUR NEIGHBORHOOD BRIGHTER

Spread happiness by creating temporary art for people in your neighborhood to enjoy. Make your own chalk paint to write words or paint pictures on a sidewalk or fence.

WHAT YOU'LL NEED

☐ ¼ cup water
☐ ¼ cup cornstarch
☐ Food coloring
☐ Paintbrush or sponge

1. Mix the water and cornstarch together.

2. Add 6 to 8 drops of food coloring and stir well.

3. Repeat steps 1 and 2 to make as many colors as you need.

4. Use a paintbrush to apply the chalk paint onto the fence or sidewalk. If you don't have a paintbrush, try a sponge.

5. If you need ideas: create abstract art made with lines and shapes; trace things like bowls, a box, or your hands; or write an encouraging message.

6. Fill in the shapes with different colors.

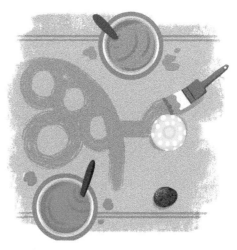

Adventure Boy Challenge

Caring for your neighborhood is a big job unless you work together with others. Organize a group of friends and family to look for and pick up trash on your block or at the local park. This will help your neighborhood stay clean and help the animals stay safe.

Getting Around

Adventure Boys can use bikes,
skateboards, in-line skates,
and scooters to get places faster.
When you are riding around you
are building muscle, balance, and
coordination that will make you
better and stronger in all
athletic activities.

SAFETY ON WHEELS

Bike and Scooter Safety: Always wear a helmet when you are on your bike or scooter. Wear bright colors so other bicyclists and cars can see you. If you are riding at night, add a light or tape a flashlight to your handlebars. You should always pay attention to and follow the rules of the road, such as stop signs and crosswalks.

Skateboard and In-line Skates Safety: To protect your body while you are on your skateboard or in-line skates, wear knee pads and elbow pads. Don't forget your helmet! Stay on the sidewalk and be on the look-out for signs that say skating is not allowed.

SO EXTREME

Did you know that cycling is an Olympic sport? There are five Olympic events that involve riding a bike.

1. Road Cycling: Racers start as a group and race a certain loop on the street.

2. Track Cycling: Bicyclists race around an oval track.

3. Cross Country Mountain Biking: Riders tackle courses on hills, forest trails, and rocky paths.

4. BMX Racing: A dirt track full of hills, jumps, and curves makes for an exciting BMX race.

5. BMX Freestyle: Riders have two minutes to perform different tricks on ramps, walls, and boxes. The judges score the winners.

Skateboarding, in the street and the park, will be in the Olympics for the first time in 2021.

CREATE YOUR OWN RACETRACK

Design your own racetrack to use with your bike, scooter, in-line skates, or skateboard and challenge yourself and your friends to conquer it.

WHAT YOU'LL NEED

- ☐ Chalk paint (page 6), sidewalk chalk, or tape
- ☐ Cones or flags (optional)
- ☐ Pool noodle, blanket, or streamers
- ☐ Stopwatch (optional)

1. Find a safe area to design the racetrack. Make sure there is enough space and that it is away from the road.

2. Decide where the start and finish lines will be. Mark them with paint, chalk, or tape.

3. Create obstacles along the racetrack.

   - Place cones, flags, or other objects that you need to go around.

   - Add a soft obstacle to duck under like a pool noodle, a blanket, or streamers.

   - Create a narrow path that you need to ride in between.

   - Paint or tape zigzags and curvy lines to ride on top of.

4. Challenge yourself and your friends to complete the track. Time each other with a stopwatch. How fast can you go? You can also try going as slow as possible.

MAKE YOUR OWN DECALS

Show off your style and personalize your wheels or helmet by making your own decals.

WHAT YOU'LL NEED

☐ Favorite pictures
☐ Scissors
☐ Markers
☐ Clear contact paper

1. First, find a picture you love. You can draw it, cut it out of a magazine, or print it from the computer.

2. Cut a piece of clear contact paper about 1 inch larger than the picture on all sides.

3. Peel the backing off the contact paper and lay it on a table, sticky-side up.

4. Place the picture facedown onto the sticky part of the contact paper.

5. Apply the decal to your bike, scooter, skateboard, or in-line skates.

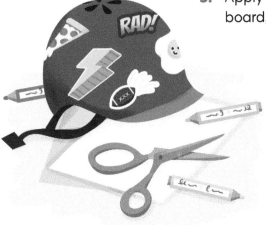

PAINT YOUR GEAR

Customize your helmet, in-line skates, or scooter with a little paint and a lot of creativity.

WHAT YOU'LL NEED

☐ Pencil
☐ Permanent marker
☐ Acrylic paint
☐ Paintbrush
☐ Painter's tape
(optional)

1. Decide what you'd like to paint. Ask an adult for permission before you start.

2. Use a pencil to draw your design on the gear so you can erase it or make changes if you need to.

3. Once you are happy with your design, trace it with a permanent marker.

4. Apply acrylic paint to add color to your design.

   Stripes: You can use painter's tape to make your lines straight by putting the tape on your gear, painting around it, and then peeling it off. Try stripes in either the same or different colors.

   Team or School Logo: Paint the logo of your favorite team or school. Print it out first and then trace it onto your gear with a pencil. Fill in the logo with paint.

   Your Name: Write your name in pencil and paint it with a bright color. You can try bubble or block letters.

SPOKE FOR YOURSELF

Make your bike stand out by adding a cool design to its spokes. Use these ideas to make your wheels more fun.

WHAT YOU'LL NEED

- ☐ Pipe cleaners
- ☐ Plastic straws
- ☐ Scissors
- ☐ Tape (optional)
- ☐ Ribbon or string
- ☐ Glow sticks

Pipe Cleaners: Wrap a pipe cleaner tightly around each bike spoke, curling it until you reach the end of the pipe cleaner. Pinch the top and bottom to secure.

Plastic Straws: Use plastic drinking straws to add color to your spokes. Cut along the entire length of one side of the straw. Open the straw and wrap it around each spoke. Use a small piece of tape in the middle of the straw to secure it, if needed. Try cutting the straws into smaller pieces and put them on your bike spokes in a pattern.

Ribbon or String: Cut ribbon or string into 5-inch pieces. Tie them onto the bike spokes in a knot. Fill up the spokes with knots of ribbon. You can also weave the ribbon through the bike spokes (over, under, over, under) and tie the ends to the spokes.

Glow Sticks: For a nighttime decoration, activate glow sticks by bending them and then weave them in and out of the bike spokes. Use string to tie them onto the spokes, if needed.

Adventure Boy Challenge

Use your initials to create your own logo. Write the letters in a bold color and add a design around them. You could add flames, lightning bolts, stripes, animals, stars, etc. Turn your logo into a decal (page 12) and put it on your bike, a notebook, or lunch box.

Dress to Express

Personalizing your clothes is a great way for Adventure Boys to show their unique style.

DESIGN YOUR CLOTHES

By adding color, patterns, or designs to plain clothes or shoes, you can turn them into something new.

WHAT YOU'LL NEED

- ☐ White clothing, such as a shirt, sneakers, canvas shoes, etc.
- ☐ Plastic garbage bag
- ☐ Permanent markers (different colors)
- ☐ Spray bottle or dropper
- ☐ Rubbing alcohol

1. Choose what you are going to customize. A white shirt, canvas sneakers, or a hat are all easy to work with.

2. Put a plastic garbage bag in between the layers of your shirt, or underneath the shoes or hat you are going to work with.

3. Draw a design on the clothing with permanent markers. Zigzags, circles, and stripes make a cool design. You don't have to color things in all the way; just scribble on the area you want to cover. You will fill in the color during the next step.

4. Use a dropper or spray bottle to apply rubbing alcohol to the design. The more alcohol you apply, the more the ink will smear and spread together. Spray until you have the effect you want.

5. Let the clothing air-dry and then put it in the clothes dryer on high for about 20 minutes to set the color.

DYE YOUR CLOTHES

Here are two very unique ways to dye your clothes. For either method, start with a piece of white clothing, like a shirt, a hat, or a pair of socks.

Make Your Own Dye

Adventure Boys can be scientists in the kitchen using leftover pieces of fruit, vegetables, and flowers to make a natural dye.

WHAT YOU'LL NEED

- ☐ 2 large or medium saucepans
- ☐ Scissors or knife (ask for an adult's permission)
- ☐ 1 cup of scraps of fruits, vegetables, or flowers
- ☐ Water
- ☐ Timer
- ☐ Spoon
- ☐ Cotton clothing or fabric
- ☐ ¼ cup salt or 1 cup vinegar
- ☐ Plastic gloves

1. Ask permission to use a saucepan. Once you use it to make dye, don't use it for cooking.

2. Decide what color of dye you'd like to make. This is where you can experiment. What can you use to get the color you want? There are a few suggestions on page 19, but you can try other combinations to see what color you get.

3. Cut the fruits, vegetables, or flowers into small pieces. You'll need 1 cup of scraps.

4. Put the chopped ingredients into the saucepan. Add enough water to cover the ingredients.

5. Ask an adult for help with this step. Turn on the stove to medium heat. Set a timer for 1 hour and let the liquid simmer. Add another cup of water if the water level gets too low.

Red
raspberries, beets,
rose petals

Orange
onion skins, carrots

Yellow
sunflowers, dandelions,
orange peels, lemon peels

Green
spinach, grass,
leaves

Blue
blueberries, blackberries,
red cabbage

Purple
purple iris,
purple cabbage

CONTINUED →

6. Turn the stove off and let the liquid cool completely. Use a spoon to scoop out the vegetables, fruits, or flowers and throw them away.

7. Use another saucepan to prepare your clothing for the dye. (You can reuse this pot for cooking in the future.) If your dye is mostly fruit, boil the clothing for 1 hour in 4 cups of water and ¼ cup of salt. If your dye is mostly vegetables, boil the clothing for 1 hour in 4 cups of water and 1 cup of vinegar.

8. After 1 hour of boiling, let the water cool completely. Rinse the clothing in cool water, then squeeze it to get the extra water out.

9. Wear plastic gloves to protect your hands and then place the clothing in the dye. You can soak the whole thing in one color or just dye half of it and then make a different colored dye to color the other half.

10. When the clothing is a color you are happy with, take it out of the dye and rinse it well with cold water. Hang the clothing up to dry.

Shibori Dyeing

Shibori is a Japanese technique of folding and gathering fabric in different ways to leave behind detailed patterns. Try just one of many techniques of Shibori dyeing, called Itajime Shibori.

WHAT YOU'LL NEED

- ☐ 1 white cotton T-shirt or pillowcase
- ☐ Scissors
- ☐ Cardboard
- ☐ Thick rubber bands
- ☐ Plastic tablecloth or old sheet
- ☐ Plastic gloves
- ☐ Denim blue fabric dye
- ☐ Water
- ☐ Large bowl or bucket
- ☐ Plastic grocery bag

1. Lay the shirt or pillowcase flat and smooth it out.

2. Starting at the bottom, fold the shirt up about 3 inches. Continue to accordion fold the shirt like a paper fan. Fold it up, flip it over, fold it up, flip it over, until you reach the top.

3. Fold in the collar and arms of the shirt so you have a long rectangle.

4. Turn the fabric rectangle so it is positioned vertically, up and down, in front of you. Start at the bottom and fold the fabric up about 3 inches. Continue to accordion fold the fabric until all you have is a square.

5. Cut two 3-inch by 3-inch cardboard squares.

6. Sandwich the folded fabric bundle between the cardboard squares. Put a thick rubber band around the fabric bundle and cardboard to hold it all together.

CONTINUED →

7. Turn the bundle and put another rubber band on, going the other way so the rubber bands cross in the middle. Repeat until you have six rubber bands crossing.

8. Protect your work space with a plastic tablecloth. You can also go outside to dye. Wear plastic gloves to protect your hands and follow the dye bottle instructions to mix the dye bath in a bowl. You might need to ask an adult for help.

9. Put the fabric bundle into the dye and move it around so it all gets submerged in the liquid.

10. Leave the fabric in the dye until it is the shade you like.

11. Gently squeeze the bundle to get any extra liquid out.

12. Put the fabric bundle in a plastic grocery bag overnight.

13. The next day, before taking the rubber bands off, rinse the shirt in cold water until the water is clear and dye isn't coming off.

14. Take the rubber bands off to reveal your new patterned shirt.

15. Wash the shirt in warm water in the washing machine and dry it in the dryer.

HISTORY OF SHIBORI

Shibori was likely introduced to Japan from China about 1,300 years ago. People without much money used it to dye cheaper fabrics like hemp because they couldn't afford cotton or silk fabric. People couldn't afford to replace their clothes very often, so they would dye them to make them look new.

Adventure Boy Challenge

Use your favorite dyeing technique to make matching shirts or pillowcases for you and a friend or sibling. Experiment with the way you fold the fabric, how you wrap it, or how many rubber bands you use.

Create Your Own Space

Sometimes Adventure Boys need a special place that they can go to relax and unwind. Make your space a place that is unique and just for you with decorations you love.

PAINT A GEOMETRIC MURAL

Add a colorful cool design to your room by painting a geometric mural.

WHAT YOU'LL NEED

☐ Butcher paper (optional)
☐ Old sheet or tarp
☐ Painter's tape
☐ Paintbrush
☐ Paint in various colors (use latex for walls or acrylic for paper)

1. Ask for permission before starting. If it isn't possible to paint on the wall, you can paint on large pieces of butcher paper and hang them up with tape to create the same effect.

2. Use an old sheet or tarp to protect the floor from paint drips.

3. Put a strip of painter's tape along the bottom, sides, and top of the walls that are next to the mural wall to keep the paint on the wall you are working on.

4. Plan a design for the wall. Try large or small triangles, zigzags, squares, or stripes. The design could cover the whole wall or just a part of it. You can mix and match shapes in your design.

5. Use the painter's tape to make the outline of the design on the wall.

6. Paint different colors inside the shapes you outlined. Don't worry if you paint over the tape. The color will not go through it.

7. Allow the paint to dry and peel the tape off.

MAKE A PILLOW

You can turn an old T-shirt you love into a new pillow for your room.

WHAT YOU'LL NEED

- ☐ Old T-shirt
- ☐ Scissors
- ☐ Hot glue gun
- ☐ Cotton balls
  (optional)

1. Decide what you love about the shirt. Is it words or a picture?

2. Lay the shirt flat and cut around the words or picture (cut the front and back of the shirt at the same time so they are the same shape).

3. The pillow can be a circle, square, oval, or a unique shape.

4. Use the hot glue gun to apply a line of glue along the edges of the bottom piece of fabric. Leave 2 inches of fabric unglued.

5. With the picture or words facing up, lay the top piece of fabric on the bottom piece and use your fingers to press along the line of glue.

6. Cut the rest of the shirt into pieces and use it as stuffing to fill the pillow. You can also use cotton balls to stuff it.

7. Glue the last section closed.

8. Find a special spot for your new pillow.

CREATE A PRIVACY NOOK

You can make your own tent to escape to for alone time, reading, writing, drawing, or even sleeping.

WHAT YOU'LL NEED

- ☐ Rope or heavy-duty string
- ☐ Blanket
- ☐ Pillows

1. Tie one end of the rope or heavy-duty string to something sturdy, like a door or closet rod.

2. Tie the other end to another sturdy piece, like a bedpost or desk. Chairs may be too light and fall over.

3. Put the blanket over the rope so that half of it is hanging on each side of the rope.

4. Create a wide area below the rope to lay on by piling up blankets and pillows to make your nook comfortable.

5. Tuck each side of the blanket underneath the pillows and blankets. This will form a tent with the blanket.

6. Add battery-operated lights or other decorations to make your nook cozy.

Adventure Boy Challenge

Make a flag for your room with an extra piece of material from an old T-shirt or sheet. Use one of the dyeing techniques (page 18) and then add a personal logo (page 15) or another design with permanent markers.

For Your Pet

It is important for Adventure
Boys to care for and be kind to
all animals, especially their pets.
Pets give us love and friendship.
It is essential that we take care of
them in return.

MAKE YOUR OWN PET TREATS

Make homemade, healthy treats for your furry friends!

WHAT YOU'LL NEED

- ☐ Bowl
- ☐ Spoon
- ☐ Baking sheet
- ☐ Parchment paper

DOG TREAT

- ☐ 1 cup all-purpose flour
- ☐ 1 cup peanut butter
- ☐ ½ cup old fashioned or rolled oats
- ☐ ½ cup water

CAT TREAT

- ☐ 1 (5-ounce) can of tuna, drained
- ☐ 1 egg
- ☐ 1¼ cups all-purpose flour
- ☐ ½ cup water

1. Preheat the oven to 350°F.

2. Combine the ingredients for the dog treats or the cat treats in a bowl. Mix them well with a spoon or your hands until they form a dough.

3. Cover a baking sheet with parchment paper.

4. Pinch off a small, marble-size piece of dough. Roll it into a ball.

5. Put the ball of dough onto the baking sheet, then press it with your fingers to flatten the ball. Repeat this step with the remaining dough.

6. Bake for 20 minutes.

7. Once the treats are cooled, keep them in a jar or bag.

ANIMAL OBSTACLE COURSE

It's time to teach your pet a few tricks! Not just how to sit or stay but also how to move through an obstacle course.

WHAT YOU'LL NEED

- ☐ Pool noodle, Hula-Hoop, or stick
- ☐ Cones or cups
- ☐ Box
- ☐ Treats

1. Start by creating one obstacle for your pet. Make sure it is a similar size to your pet.

2. You can use a pool noodle, a Hula-Hoop, or a stick for your pet to jump over. Put out cones or cups for your pet to weave around. Use a box, with both ends open, as a tunnel for your pet to go through.

3. Hold a treat in your hand to lead your pet through the obstacle. You could also put different treats on the ground along the way to lead your pet through it.

4. After your pet has completed the obstacle a few times with treats, add a command with your voice or hand to go along with the treats.

5. Always give your pet praise and encouragement. If an obstacle seems too hard or overwhelming for your pet, make the task shorter and simpler, and encourage them along the way.

6. After your pet has learned how to do one obstacle, it will become the last obstacle in your course. Add a new obstacle in front of it. For example, if your pet has learned to jump over a pool noodle, add a cup in front of the noodle to go around before jumping over the noodle. This is called back-chaining. You are teaching the last obstacles first and working your way toward the beginning of the course.

MAKE YOUR OWN PET TOYS

Adventure Boys spend quality time with their pets! Make a toy for your pet that they will love.

Dog Toy

WHAT YOU'LL NEED

☐ Plastic water bottle
☐ 1 long sock, like a tube sock

1. Push an empty plastic water bottle into a long sock, all the way to the end of the sock.

2. Tie a knot at the open end of the sock.

3. Use this toy to play tug-o-war or fetch. Your dog will love the crinkling sound it makes.

Cat Toy

☐ Scissors
☐ Paper towel tube
☐ Cat treats or catnip

1. Cut a paper towel tube in half.

2. Tuck a few cat treats or catnip inside one half of the tube.

3. Fold both ends in toward the middle.

4. Shake the toy and challenge your cat to get the treats out.

Rabbit and Guinea Pig Toy

☐ Scissors
☐ Paper towel tube
☐ Carrots and lettuce
☐ Hay

1. Cut a hole in the middle of a paper towel tube.

2. Put pieces of carrots and lettuce through the hole into the middle of the tube.

3. Stuff hay into each end of the tube to hold the vegetables in the middle.

4. Give the toy to your rabbit or guinea pig. Watch them try to get to the middle where the tasty treats are.

Adventure Boy Challenge

Make dog or cat treats (page 29) for your neighbors' pets. Write a note to go with the treats that includes the ingredient list so they know what they are feeding their pet. Deliver them to spread kindness.

Balloon Power

Wind is a powerful energy source. Windmills or turbines use wind to make energy for pumping water or providing electricity. Using a balloon, let's experiment with how wind can power different things.

BALLOON TORPEDO

Let's use wind to power a torpedo and send it flying.

WHAT YOU'LL NEED

- ☐ Balloon
- ☐ Drinking straw
- ☐ Small rubber band
- ☐ Scissors
- ☐ Card stock
- ☐ Tape

1. Attach a balloon to the end of a straw with a rubber band.

2. Cut four small ½-inch by 2-inch rectangles from card stock to make fins on the bottom of the torpedo.

3. Tape the rectangles to the bottom of the straw so that they make an X. Leave a bit of room on the end of the straw, below the fins, so you can blow up the balloon.

4. As you blow up the balloon, it might be helpful to hold it on the section that's secured by the rubber band.

5. Pinch the straw to keep the air inside of the balloon.

6. Find an open space to let your torpedo fly.

Fun Tip: See if you can change how your torpedo flies by changing the size of the balloon, straw, or fins. Make one adjustment at a time and experiment.

BALLOON RACERS

Let's use wind to power a car and have a race.

WHAT YOU'LL NEED

- ☐ Scissors
- ☐ Cardboard
- ☐ 3 straws
- ☐ Tape
- ☐ Nail (ask for an adult's permission)
- ☐ 4 plastic bottle caps or craft foam
- ☐ 4 toothpicks
- ☐ Balloon
- ☐ Rubber band

1. Cut a piece of cardboard into a 3-inch by 5-inch rectangle.

2. Cut two straws to the exact width of the rectangle, about 3 inches.

3. Tape a straw to each end of the cardboard rectangle.

4. Use a nail to carefully poke a small hole in the middle of each bottle cap. You might need to ask an adult for help. If you don't have bottle caps, you can cut craft foam into circles.

5. Put a toothpick into the straw on each side and tape it to the straw.

6. Slide the bottle cap wheels onto the toothpicks.

7. You've made the car, so now let's add wind power to it. Cut a third straw in half. Attach a balloon to one end of the straw and use a rubber band to secure it.

8. Tape the straw to the top of the cardboard, making sure to leave a little bit hanging over the edge so you can use it to blow up the balloon.

9. Your wind-powered car is ready to go. Hold the car with your fingers on the straw. Use the straw to blow up the balloon and cover the straw with your fingers to keep the air in the balloon.

10. Put the car on the floor. Remove your fingers and let the wind power move the car.

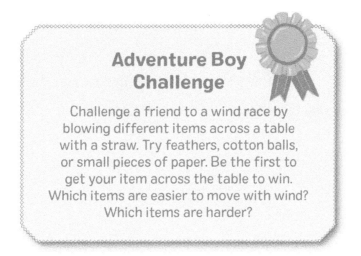

Adventure Boy Challenge

Challenge a friend to a wind race by blowing different items across a table with a straw. Try feathers, cotton balls, or small pieces of paper. Be the first to get your item across the table to win. Which items are easier to move with wind? Which items are harder?

A Nature Hideaway

Building a shelter is a great skill for Adventure Boys to have. You can use a shelter to protect yourself from weather, as a place to relax, or as a clubhouse for your friends and siblings.

KEEP IN MIND

Choose a dry spot to build your shelter. Build up the floor of your shelter so it is off the ground. This will keep you warm and dry. You can use a layer of sticks topped with grasses and leaves, or you can layer a thick pile of leaves on the ground.

Be aware of animals and insects that are living in or around the branches, sticks, and leaves that you collect. Be able to identify poison ivy and poison oak, and make sure not to touch those plants. If possible, look for sticks and branches to use that have already fallen. You don't want to harm a tree by cutting or ripping off its branches.

MAKE A NATURE SHELTER

You can build a shelter quickly, or you can make it perfect just for you.

WHAT YOU'LL NEED

- ☐ Trees
- ☐ Thick rope
- ☐ Large sticks or branches, at least 4 feet long
- ☐ Grasses or leaves

1. Look for two trees that are 4 to 6 feet apart.

2. Tie the rope around one tree trunk about 4 feet above the ground. Pull the rope tightly to the next tree and tie it around that tree trunk. Make sure your rope is secure.

3. Gather long sticks or branches that have already fallen from trees.

CONTINUED →

4. Lean the sticks and branches on the rope at an angle. Leave a few inches of the sticks above the rope in case it is windy or gets bumped.

5. Continue to balance sticks along the rope until you have a solid wall. Cover any openings with grass, leaves, or smaller sticks.

6. Lay a row of sticks on the floor of your shelter and cover them with leaves. If you don't have enough sticks, lay a thick layer of leaves or a tarp to keep you dry and warm.

7. If you don't have access to a forest, build your shelter in the corner of a fenced-in area by tying the rope to the fence on each side of the corner.

BUILD A TREE HOUSE

Work with an adult to construct a tree house that you can spend time in.

WHAT YOU'LL NEED

- ☐ Tree
- ☐ Power drill or hammer
- ☐ 2 (6-foot) pieces of treated lumber (2-inch by 6-inch or larger)
- ☐ 28 (8-inch) screws or nails
- ☐ Level
- ☐ Tape measure
- ☐ Saw
- ☐ 2 (3-foot) pieces of treated lumber (2-inch by 6-inch or larger)
- ☐ 8 (4-foot) pieces of treated lumber (1-inch by 6-inch or larger)
- ☐ 40 (3-inch) screws or nails

1. Choose a strong tree with branches that start higher up so there is room for your tree house without having to cut any branches.

2. Using a drill or hammer, attach one (6-foot) piece of wood to each side of the tree (about 4 to 6 feet above the ground) with an 8-inch screw or nail.

3. Use a level to make sure the boards are both even and straight. Then, put in four more screws or nails through each board and into the tree to secure.

CONTINUED →

4. Measure the width between each board. Cut two (3-foot) boards to that size. Slide them between the main boards, against the tree. Using four or five (8-inch) screws or nails, attach those boards to the tree.

5. Use two more 8-inch screws or nails to go through the main boards on each side, into the cross boards. Now you have a solid base for your tree house.

6. Arrange the 4-foot boards along the top of the base as your decking. It is okay to have spacing between the boards. That way it will be easier to keep clean.

7. Use 3-inch screws or nails to attach the decking boards to the base.

8. There will still be two sides of the tree that don't have any decking. Add a few pieces of decking on the back of the tree and leave the front open for climbing up and entering the tree house.

9. Install a ladder with extra wood pieces and 8-inch screws or nails, or attach a climbing rope.

Adventure Boy Challenge

Customize your own walking stick. Find a solid stick that is taller than your waist. Paint your walking stick with acrylic paint and take it with you on your hiking adventures.

Clay Crafts

From characters and games to bowls and plates, sculpting clay is a skill that Adventure Boys can use for many things.

TYPES OF CLAY

Clay comes from the earth as rocks are broken down by the weather over time. Most types of clay need a kiln (a special high-temperature oven for pottery), but there are three types of clay that you can work with at home that don't need a kiln.

Polymer Clay: It is soft, brightly colored, and hardens in the oven.

Air-Dry Modeling Clay: It shrinks slightly as it dries over time and can be painted after it hardens.

Pottery Clay: A natural clay that can be cured in a kiln but will also harden if it is left out to dry. It is usually a shade of brown and can be painted after it hardens.

MAKE A LEAF BOWL

Make leaf bowls of different shapes, sizes, and colors for decoration or as a gift.

WHAT YOU'LL NEED

☐ Leaves
☐ Wax paper
☐ Air-dry modeling clay
☐ Rolling pin
☐ Butter knife
☐ Bowl
☐ Paintbrush
☐ Acrylic paint

1. Find a leaf with a shape that you like and that also has a lot of veins (lines) on the back of it.

2. Protect your work surface with a piece of wax paper.

3. Take a handful of air-dry modeling clay and put it on the wax paper. Use a rolling pin to roll it out until it is evenly flattened and about ¼-inch thick.

4. Put the leaf onto the middle of the clay. Gently press the leaf into the clay with the rolling pin.

5. Using a butter knife, trim away the extra clay around the leaf. Remove the leaf from the clay.

6. Lift the leaf-shaped clay up with the wax paper under it. Set the wax paper and leaf into a bowl so it curves like the bowl. If the leaf is smaller than the bowl, use aluminum foil to make a smaller bowl for your leaf to sit in.

7. Let your leaf bowl dry and harden, remove it from the wax paper, and paint it.

Steps 1–3

Step 4

Step 5

Step 6

Step 7

POLYMER CLAY ANIMALS

Make your own animals, characters, or creatures out of polymer clay.

WHAT YOU'LL NEED

- ☐ Polymer clay (different colors)
- ☐ Toothpick or fork
- ☐ Baking sheet

1. Decide what type of animal or character you are going to make and what colors you want it to be. Roll a piece of clay into a circle or oval shape to form the body.

2. Roll a smaller circle for the head and press it onto the body.

3. Make different shapes, such as triangles or cylinders, to add legs, a tail, ears, and eyes.

4. Use a toothpick or a fork to poke the clay to create different details, such as eyes, lines, or hair.

5. Gently place the clay animals onto a baking sheet. Follow the instructions on the clay package to bake your creations.

Adventure Boy Challenge

Make a tic-tac-toe game out of polymer clay. Sculpt two different sets of characters or shapes that look the same. Make a tic-tac-toe board out of clay, or play on a piece of paper with your new game pieces.

Paper Projects

From papier-mâché and airplanes
to origami and homemade paper,
the possibilities of what you can
create with paper are endless!

MAKE A PAPIER-MÂCHÉ MASK

Create a papier-mâché mask to wear as a costume or to hang in your room as a decoration.

WHAT YOU'LL NEED

- ☐ Scissors
- ☐ Cardboard
- ☐ Tape
- ☐ Plastic tablecloth or old sheet
- ☐ Newspaper
- ☐ 2 cups flour
- ☐ 1 cup water
- ☐ Bowl
- ☐ Printer paper (optional)
- ☐ Paint, sequins, feathers, or other decorations

1. Create the basic shape of a mask using cardboard pieces and tape. Bend it, piece it together, and secure it with tape. You can leave a space for eyes or a mouth. If you are going to wear the mask, make a hole on each side so you can add a string later.

2. Protect your work surface with a plastic table-cloth or old sheet.

3. Rip newspaper into 1-inch strips.

4. Mix the flour and water in a bowl.

5. Dip a strip of newspaper in the mixture until it is completely soaked and lay it on the card-board mask. If the ends hang off the edge of the mask, fold them around the back.

CONTINUED →

6. Continue layering the strips of paper in different directions, making sure the strips overlap each other. Once you have five layers of paper, let the mask dry for a few hours.

7. Add five more layers of soaked newspaper, for a total of 10 layers. For the last layer, cover the mask with strips of white printer paper (optional).

8. Let the mask dry overnight.

9. Use paint, sequins, feathers, or yarn to decorate your mask.

MAKE YOUR OWN PAPER

Paper is made from pieces of a tree that are turned into pulp and then pressed flat. In a factory, a machine is used to speed up the process. However, you can make your own paper without a machine.

WHAT YOU'LL NEED

- ☐ Scissors
- ☐ Scraps of white or colored paper
- ☐ Bowl
- ☐ Water
- ☐ Blender (ask an adult for assistance)
- ☐ Grease splatter screen
- ☐ Baking sheet
- ☐ Spoon or pan (optional)
- ☐ Dish towels (optional)

1. Cut or rip paper into tiny ½-inch pieces. Put the pieces of paper into a bowl and cover them with water. Let the paper soak for a couple of hours, or until it is soggy.

2. Pour the paper and water into a blender and blend until it becomes a thick pulp. If it is too dry, add more water.

3. Balance a grease splatter screen on top of a baking sheet. Scoop the pulp onto the top of the splatter screen.

4. Use your hands, a spoon, or the bottom of a pan to press the pulp together so that it forms a sheet. You want the sheet of pulp to be just thick enough to stay together but look like a piece of paper.

CONTINUED →

5. As you press the pulp, it will also squeeze the water out of the pulp and onto the baking sheet. You want to squeeze as much water out as you can. You can put a dish towel over the top of the pulp as you press down to help soak up the water.

6. Flip the layer of pulp onto a flat surface to air-dry.

7. Once it is dry, use scissors to trim the edges of the paper to make them even if you wish.

8. Use the paper to write a note, draw a picture, or make bookmarks.

Adventure Boy Challenge

Make a paper gift that can turn into flowers. After blending the pulp of the paper, add a packet of flower seeds. Then, make your paper into a card, ornament, or bookmark. Give it as a gift and let the person know the paper can be planted in the ground to grow beautiful flowers.

Tell Your Story

Storytelling is an art that has been around for thousands of years. Stories were shared with words, pictures, and eventually on paper. Adventure Boys can use a story to share an experience, teach a lesson, or make someone laugh.

STORYTELLING BASICS

When you are writing a story, it is important for it to be planned out and organized. It needs a beginning, middle, and end that flow together smoothly. A great story also needs:

1. **Setting:** Where and when is your story happening?

2. **Characters:** Who is the story is about? The most important characters are the main characters.

3. **Problem or Conflict:** What is the problem in the story? Usually the conflict happens to the main characters.

4. **Solution:** How does the problem get solved? Sometimes the solution is quick, and sometimes it takes longer to tell how the conflict gets resolved.

STORY STICKS

Make a set of story sticks that you can use to create exciting stories.

WHAT YOU'LL NEED

- ☐ Craft sticks
- ☐ Pen
- ☐ Markers (different colors)
- ☐ Cup

1. Brainstorm a list of 10 places a story could take place, such as the forest, a desert, or an empty cave. Write the name of each place on the bottom of a craft stick. Color the top of those craft sticks blue.

2. Think of 10 different characters that could be in a story, such as a king, an animal, or a wizard. Color the top of those craft sticks yellow and write a character on each one.

3. Write 10 problems of a story on the bottom of craft sticks, such as someone is lost, something is broken, or a dragon is in the way. Color the top of those sticks red.

4. Color the top of 10 craft sticks green and write solutions on the bottom of each stick. The solutions don't need to match the problems you picked. They can be things such as magic, saved by a hero, or people learn a lesson.

5. Put the sticks in a cup with the colors at the top.

6. Pick a blue, yellow, red, and green stick. Write a story with them and add other details.

ROCK PAINTING STORY

Before people started writing stories with words, they told stories with pictures. Adventure Boys can use pictures to tell stories, too.

WHAT YOU'LL NEED

- ☐ Paper
- ☐ Pen
- ☐ Rocks
- ☐ Paintbrush
- ☐ Acrylic paint or paint pens
- ☐ Glue and water (optional)

1. On a piece of paper, write a short story, about 10 sentences long. Make sure your story has a setting, characters, a problem, and a solution.

2. Gather a rock for each sentence of your story, about 10 rocks total.

3. Think of a picture that could represent each sentence and paint them on the rocks.

4. Let the paint dry. You can seal the rocks to protect your picture with a mixture of equal parts glue and water.

5. Tell your story to a friend or sibling by setting out one rock at a time.

6. Challenge a friend or sibling to make up a different story to tell using your rocks.

Adventure Boy Challenge

Use the story sticks with a friend or sibling. Pick four sticks and use those details in a story you tell together. Take turns adding a sentence to the story. Tell your story aloud or write it down.

Feel the Beat

Music spreads joy and gets
your body moving, but did you
know that making music is
also good for your brain?

MAKE A FINGER PIANO

A finger piano is a percussion instrument that was invented in Africa thousands of years ago. Make your own finger piano in a few simple steps. Ask an adult for permission and for help using the staple gun.

WHAT YOU'LL NEED

- ☐ Small piece of wood
- ☐ 5 bobby pins
- ☐ Staple gun
- ☐ Hammer

1. Find a scrap piece of wood that is about 3 inches by 5 inches.

2. Unbend and straighten five bobby pins. Spread them out evenly on the wood, with one end of the bobby pins lining up with the edge of the wood.

3. Use the staple gun to put a staple on top of each bobby pin, close to the edge of the wood. Put the first staple in the same spot for each bobby pin so they are all in a row.

4. Hammer the staples into the wood to secure them, if needed.

CONTINUED →

5. Staple each bobby pin again. This time, each staple should move up slightly from the previous one, so they are in a diagonal line. Hammer those staples down to secure them, if needed.

6. Lift the end of each bobby pin so it bends up. Test out the notes by pushing down each bobby pin with your fingers.

7. To change the pitch, make the part of the bobby pin that sticks up shorter by adding more staples.

MÂCHÉ MARACAS

Maracas were originally made in Puerto Rico with the dried round fruit from the Higuera tree. Make your own maracas using the papier-mâché technique you learned earlier (page 51).

WHAT YOU'LL NEED

☐ Funnel
☐ Rice or beans
☐ 2 balloons
☐ 2 cups (for balancing the balloons)
☐ 2 cups flour
☐ 1 cup water
☐ Bowl
☐ Paper, either news-paper or copy paper
☐ Glue or string
☐ 2 sticks
☐ Paintbrush
☐ Paint

1. Use a funnel to put a handful of rice or beans into two balloons.

2. Blow up the balloons to about the same size and tie them. Balance each balloon on the top of a cup, with the knot inside the cup.

3. Mix the flour and water in a bowl. Rip strips of paper and dip them into the mixture.

4. Cover the top half of the balloons with strips of paper, crossing the strips over each other in different directions, until you have five layers. Let them dry overnight.

5. Flip the balloons over so that the papier-mâché side is in the cup. Tie or glue a stick onto the knot of each balloon.

6. Add five layers of papier-mâché over the bottom of the balloons and top of the sticks. This will help keep the sticks straight and sturdy. Let them dry.

7. Once they're dry, paint your maracas.

DRUMS

The drum sets the rhythm of a song and leads the rest of the musicians, which makes the drummer really important! Test out three different ways to make a drum to see which sound you like the best.

WHAT YOU'LL NEED

☐ Cylinder container
☐ Lids, balloons and rubber bands, or packaging tape
☐ Packaging tape

1. Find a cylinder container. It can be metal, plastic, or cardboard.

2. There are three options for drum tops:

   • **Lids:** If your container comes with a lid, keep it on and secure it with tape.

   • **Balloons:** Cut the top of a balloon off and slide the bottom of the balloon (the larger piece) over the top of the container. Put a rubber band around the edge of the container to keep the balloon on.

   • **Tape:** Attach strips of tape to the top of the container and over the edges, making an X. Keep adding strips of tape that cross in the middle until the entire surface is covered. Add two layers of tape.

3. You can beat the drum with your hands or use drumsticks (page 65).

Drumsticks

☐ Tissue paper
☐ 2 pencils
☐ Packaging tape

1. Crumple a piece of tissue paper into a ball at the top of a pencil.

2. Cover the tissue paper ball with pieces of packaging tape that overlap the ball and top of the pencil. This will keep the ball securely attached to the pencil. Keep adding tape until it is completely covered.

3. Use your drumsticks to make a beat on a drum.

MUSIC OF THE WORLD

Music is an art, and people have been playing instruments for thousands of years. The oldest instrument is the flute. It was originally made from animal bones. The finger piano, also called a kalimba or mbira, was invented in Africa. Maracas were invented in Puerto Rico, and the bongo drum is from Cuba. The modern guitar that is still used today was made in Spain, and the piano came from Italy. No matter where you are in the world, music is a thing that ALL people have in common!

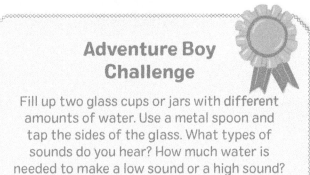

Adventure Boy Challenge

Fill up two glass cups or jars with different amounts of water. Use a metal spoon and tap the sides of the glass. What types of sounds do you hear? How much water is needed to make a low sound or a high sound? Experiment with different amounts of water and the sounds you can create.

That's Entertainment

Now it's time to use your talents to put on a show for your friends and family! Perform a play that shares a story you came up with, or create music with instruments. Adventure Boys are artistic and skillful.

PUT ON A PLAY

You can turn a story that you've written into a play! Use the storytelling tips (page 57) to make sure your play includes all of the elements it needs. You can also use the story sticks (page 58) to create a new story for your play.

Write Your Play

The narrator is the person who will be in charge of telling the story to the audience while the characters act out what's happening in the story. Decide which parts you want the narrator to read.

How many people do you need to perform in your play? Ask your friends and family if they'd like to be a part of the performance. Do each of your characters have a speaking part? If not and you want them to, you can always add that to your play.

Set the Stage

Whether you perform your play inside or outside, clear a space that will become your stage. Create an area for the audience to sit, such as blankets, chairs, or the couch. Make tickets to your play that the audience can use to enter. You can also make a program that includes the title of your play, the names of the people playing each character, and other people who helped with the play.

CONTINUED →

Costumes and Props

A simple costume can turn your friends and family into the characters they are pretending to be. Make your own costumes using a hat, glasses, a fake mustache, or a wig. You can use a bed sheet or towel and tape to make different types of clothes, such as a dress or robe. Use paper, cardboard, or papier-mâché (page 51) to make props that will help the characters share the story.

Adventure Boy Challenge

Write a review that could appear online or in a newspaper about the performance of your play or about the music your band plays together. What was the best part? What did the audience say?

START A BACKYARD BAND

Grab a few friends and family members to start your own band. You can play instruments that you've made or use ones you've already been practicing.

- Decide how many band members you need.

- As a group, decide what type of music the band will play. Will you write your own songs or play songs that are already known?

- Brainstorm and vote on a name for your band.

- Practice, practice, practice!

- When your band is ready to perform a few songs, invite your friends and family to a performance.

Getting Physical

Get outside and play a game with friends, Adventure Boy! Not only will you have fun, but exercise is good for your muscles and your brain, too!

CREATE YOUR OWN SPORT

You can create your own sport to play with your friends and family.

1. Decide if your game is going to be played with a ball, a stick, or just with people.

2. Think about one or two things you like about your favorite sport and use it in the new sport you are creating.

3. How many players will you need?

4. How does the game start? How do you win?

5. What rules do you need to keep it fair?

6. Write down the rules of your game and teach a friend how to play.

A NEW TWIST ON AN OLD GAME

The game of HORSE has been around for many years. I bet your parents used to play it when they were your age! Ask friends or family members to join you for a game.

WHAT YOU'LL NEED

☐ Basketball
☐ Basketball hoop

1. Player 1 starts as the leader and shoots the ball at the hoop from anywhere. If player 1 makes the shot, the other players have to try to make it from the same spot. If they don't make it, they get a letter (starting with H) to start spelling the word HORSE.

2. If player 1 doesn't make the shot, then it is player 2's turn to be the leader and shoot the ball from anywhere.

3. If player 2 makes the shot, then the other players try to make it from the same spot. They get a letter if they miss. If player 2 doesn't make the shot, it is player 3's turn to be the leader.

4. Keep taking turns, and any player who gets all of the letters to spell the word HORSE is out. The last player left in the game is the winner!

Twists on the Game

- Add a rule that if the leader makes their shot and then all of the other players make the same shot, the leader gets a letter.
- Add a rule that if the leader makes two shots in a row, that their next shot has to be a trick shot, such as backward over their head, from behind the hoop, or bouncing the ball to get it in.
- Use a smaller ball, such as a tennis ball, to play the game.

Adventure Boy Challenge

Organize a tournament for your friends and family where they will play either HORSE, the new sport you invented, or another favorite game. Play 10 times over several days or weeks and keep track of who wins each game. Make a trophy for the winner.

Seeing Through a New Lens

You can look through the lens of a camera to take a picture or use a periscope to look around without being seen. Making videos is another way to look through a lens. No matter what type of lens you are using, Adventure Boys can discover new things to see and share with others.

MAKE YOUR OWN CAMERA

Make your own camera obscura, or pinhole camera, and experiment with light and how a camera works.

WHAT YOU'LL NEED

□ Wax paper
□ 2 toilet paper tubes
□ Rubber bands
□ Aluminum foil
□ Pin or nail (ask for an adult's permission)
□ Tape

1. Fit a piece of wax paper tightly over the end of one toilet paper tube. Wrap a rubber band around the tube to secure it.

2. Fit a piece of aluminum foil tightly over the end of the other toilet paper tube. Wrap a rubber band around the tube to secure it.

3. Use a pin to poke a hole in the middle of the aluminum foil.

4. Put the aluminum foil end of the tube on the table. Put the wax paper end of the other tube on top of the foil tube. Tape them together.

5. Roll the pinhole camera (except the ends) in aluminum foil and tape to secure it.

6. Now experiment with the pinhole camera. Point it toward a light or take it outside and look around. Look into the open end and point the pinhole toward what you want to see.

7. The images will appear upside down. In a camera, the film would be where your eye is and the image would be recorded on it.

PERISCOPE

A periscope can be used to look over a wall or around corners without being seen. A submarine uses a periscope to look just above the water for any targets or threats. Make your own periscope and use it in your nature shelter (page 39) or tree house (page 41).

WHAT YOU'LL NEED

☐ Toothpaste box
☐ Tape
☐ Pencil
☐ Ruler
☐ Box cutter (ask an adult for assistance)
☐ Scissors
☐ 2 small mirrors, about 2 inches in diameter
☐ Marker

1. Tape both ends of an empty toothpaste box closed.

2. On the bottom of one side of the box, trace a square that would fit one of the small mirrors.

3. Ask an adult for help using a box cutter to cut the top line that you traced.

4. Using scissors, cut the lines on the sides. Do not cut the bottom line (the line closest to the end) that you traced.

5. Fold the flap inside the box until it touches the other side. Attach a piece of tape so it stays folded inward.

6. Flip the box to the other side and trace a square to fit the other mirror on the opposite end of the box.

7. Ask an adult for help cutting the top line with a box cutter, and use scissors to cut the lines on the sides. Do not cut the bottom line that you traced.

8. Fold the flap inside the box and tape it to the other side.

9. Attach a mirror to each flap with a loop of tape so they are at a 45-degree angle.

10. Look into the bottom mirror of the periscope. What do you see?

11. Experiment with different size boxes and mirrors. Tape two boxes together to make a longer periscope. Does it change how it works?

Tip: Your mirror does not need to be the same width as your box.

MAKE A MUSIC VIDEO

A music video can tell the story of what a song is about or feature a band playing and singing a song in a fun way.

WHAT YOU'LL NEED

☐ Smartphone, tablet, or laptop
☐ Video editing app

1. Plan your music video. What song will you use? What costumes will you wear? Where will you record it?

2. Practice before you record. Practicing is important because it gives everyone a chance to know what the others are planning to do, where they will move, and the person shooting the video will know where to focus the camera.

3. Record your performance with a smartphone, tablet, or laptop.

4. If you need to, you can edit your music video using an editing app, such as iMovie, Animotica, or Magisto. Ask an adult or friend for help with this step as you learn how to edit and get used to the app.

5. Have a video watching party to enjoy your new music video.

> **Fun Tip:** Make a video of your band performing with their new instruments.

MAKE A STOP-MOTION VIDEO

Stop-motion animation is a video story made from a series of pictures. You can use stop-motion animation to make characters and objects that cannot move on their own appear to move. For example, you can make a stuffed animal or toy seem like it is walking. You can make a drawing of a person appear to dance.

WHAT YOU'LL NEED

☐ Computer, tablet, or smartphone
☐ Stop-motion app (there are many free apps available)
☐ Toy character, such as a Lego character, stuffed animal, dinosaur, etc.)
☐ Background image

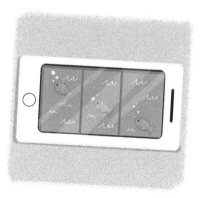

1. Ask an adult to use a device such as a computer, tablet, or smartphone. Agree on a free stop-motion app to download and use.

2. Decide which toy character you'd like to use to make a stop-motion video. You could use a Lego character, stuffed animal, or another toy.

3. The background of a stop-motion video can be really important. You want a background image that stays the same for each picture and that is big enough to fill the screen on your device.

4. Make a plan for your character. Is it going to dance, walk, run, or climb?

5. In your stop-motion app, arrange your character in front of the background and take the first picture.

CONTINUED →

6. Move your character slightly and take another picture.

7. Continue moving your character just a little bit and taking pictures each time you move it.

8. When your character has gotten to the end of the movement, take the last picture and push done or finish in your app to create a movie.

> **Keep in Mind:** If you aren't happy with your first video, try again! It takes a little practice to make a video with a smooth flow.
>
> **Fun Tip:** Once you've gotten stop-motion down, try using more than one character.

Adventure Boy Challenge

Use modeling clay to create characters for a stop-motion video. You will be able to move the clay to change the character's expression or how it is posed to tell your story.

Share with the World

Sharing ideas, talents, and even things you own makes the world a better place. Start by sharing with your friends and family and then even your neighborhood and city.

CREATE A NEIGHBORHOOD BOOK EXCHANGE

Sharing books is one way that Adventure Boys can share with their community. Organize a way for the people in your neighborhood to share books.

1. Decide on a location for your book exchange. It can be at the end of your driveway, at a mailbox, or outside of a business. (Make sure to ask for permission from the business owner first!)

2. To store the books, you can decorate a plastic storage tub, paint an old cabinet, or build a wooden box. Make sure it is able to protect the books from rain.

3. Make a flyer to pass out to your neighbors explaining your mission of building a neighborhood book exchange, where it will be located, and ask for book donations to help get it started.

4. Make a sign for the book exchange that encourages neighbors (both adults and kids) to take and leave books. Make sure to include that it is free to use.

MAKE A DOCUMENTARY

A documentary is a way that you can share information. You can feature your neighborhood and the people in it, spotlight school events, or explain facts about something interesting.

Documentary Ideas

- Interview someone who has lived in the area for a long time about how the neighborhood has changed.

- Talk to local store owners about what they offer and ways they help your neighborhood.

- Talk to someone who has an interesting hobby or is an expert on a certain subject.

- Share details about events that have happened during a school year.

Asking Permission

Make sure you ask people who you are interviewing or businesses that you are talking about for permission to be included in your documentary. Tell them what your documentary is about and with whom or where you plan to share it.

Filming and Editing

1. Use a smartphone, laptop, or tablet to record your documentary.

2. Record the conversation between yourself and the person or people you are interviewing. Make sure to ask questions and respond in a respectful way.

3. Take videos of places, pictures, or other things that go with the topic of your documentary. This is called "B-roll," which means it's not the main interview subject, but supporting images. B-roll makes your documentary more interesting to watch, as when you edit, you'll switch between these images and the interviews. It is okay to stop recording between each part because you can edit them together later.

4. Use a video editing app, such as iMovie, Animotica, or Magisto, to blend together the pieces of video you recorded. Ask an adult for help as you learn how to edit and get used to the app.

RECORD A PODCAST

A podcast shares information like a documentary, but it is something that you listen to instead of watch.

1. Decide on a topic you know a lot about and are excited to discuss.

2. Research to learn as much as you can about your topic. Read books, look for articles on the internet, or watch a documentary.

3. Make a list of things you want to talk about. These are called talking points. You can refer to your talking points to keep you on topic during the podcast.

4. Use a voice memo app on a smartphone, tablet, or laptop to record your podcast to share with friends and family.

5. If you discover that you are really interested in making podcasts and want to make a series of them, you could use an app such as GarageBand or Audacity. You would be able to record, edit, add music and an introduction, all on the same app.

Adventure Boy Challenge

Interview as many older family members as you can (parents, grandparents, cousins, aunts, and uncles) and ask them what it was like when they were your age. What was their favorite game, favorite school memory, and favorite holiday tradition? Make a documentary to share what you've learned and have a family party to watch it together.

Design a Game

Adventures boys are smart, inventive, and like to have fun. Use your skills to make a board game so that everyone can have fun together. You can even host a game night where everyone brings a game that they've made themselves.

MAKE YOUR OWN BOARD GAME

WHAT YOU'LL NEED

- ☐ Cardboard or paper
- ☐ Tape
- ☐ Markers
- ☐ Glue
- ☐ Stickers (optional)
- ☐ Dice or other game pieces (optional)
- ☐ Modeling clay (optional)

1. Figure out the goal of your board game. Will it be to collect the most of something, to get to the finish line first, or to answer the most questions correctly?

2. Decide if your game will use dice, cards, or both.

3. Create a theme for your game and design a game board. Use cardboard or tape pieces of paper together to make the board.

4. Add details to your game with markers, paper and glue, or stickers. Make cards if needed.

5. Write a set of rules, including how to start and how a player wins.

6. Use game pieces like dice from another game, turn small toys into game pieces, or make your own out of modeling clay.

Adventure Boy Challenge

Use your video skills (page 85) to make and record a commercial for your game. Include the name of the game, the directions, how you win, and why you'd recommend it.

Take Care of the Planet

Taking care of the planet is one way that Adventure Boys can make a difference. Reusing items that would normally get thrown away is a skill that you can practice and teach to others.

REPURPOSE OLD JEANS

Take an old pair of jeans that you can't wear anymore and turn them into beanbags.

WHAT YOU'LL NEED

- ☐ Old jeans
- ☐ Scissors
- ☐ Ruler
- ☐ Marker
- ☐ Hot glue gun
- ☐ Funnel
- ☐ Beans or rice

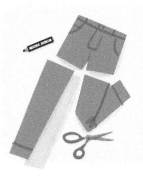

1. Take an old pair of jeans and cut the legs off. Cut up along both seams of the jeans to separate the fabric. Measure and cut out 5-inch squares.

2. On the inside of the fabric, use a marker to draw a square with the lines about a half inch away from the edge.

3. Use the glue gun to apply glue along three sides of the bottom square, leaving one side unglued. Put the top piece of fabric on top and press together with your fingers.

4. Use a funnel to fill the bean bag with rice or beans.

5. Carefully apply another line of glue to seal the fourth side closed.

CONTINUED →

6. Press the lines of glue as they cool, and your beanbag is ready!

7. You can make different shaped beanbags, too! Try triangles, circles, or even stars, and make them big or small.

Fun Tip: Cut around the outside of each jean pocket to make something new. Attach them to a bulletin board to organize toys or markers. Glue them to another piece of fabric to make a tool belt. What else can you do with them?

PLASTIC BOTTLE WATER MAZE

Make your own water maze from empty plastic bottles and experiment with changing the path of water.

WHAT YOU'LL NEED

- ☐ Plastic bottles and containers
- ☐ Scissors
- ☐ Hole punch
- ☐ Zip ties or twine
- ☐ Water

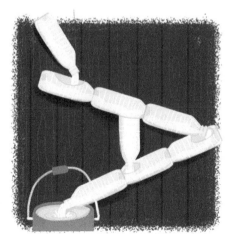

1. Collect plastic bottles and containers of all shapes and sizes. Remove and recycle any caps and lids.

2. Find a place to make your water maze. Try a fence, a deck railing, or a gate.

3. Using scissors, carefully cut a golf ball–size hole in the first bottle. You might need to ask an adult for help.

4. Punch two holes near the opening you cut. Lace a zip tie or piece of twine through the two holes and tie the bottle to the fence. This will be the beginning of your water maze, so start as high up the fence as you can.

5. Take another bottle and cut a hole in the side. Figure out where the bottle needs to be so the water can flow from the first bottle into the second bottle. Make sure the bottle is tilted so the water will flow down. Punch two holes and tie that bottle into place.

CONTINUED →

6. Take another bottle and cut a hole in the side. This time, have it face the opposite direction to send the water a different way. Punch two holes and attach it to the fence.

7. Continue cutting holes into containers and bottles and arranging them so the water will travel through from the beginning to the end of the maze. Test each bottle before you attach it so you can make sure the water will fall into the next bottle accurately.

8. Pour water at the top and watch it flow. Add as many containers as you can to make a zigzagging water maze.

CEREAL BOX CITY

Create a city out of cereal boxes and containers. It can be a model of the city you live in, or a place for your characters to live and cars to drive through.

WHAT YOU'LL NEED

- ☐ Cardboard boxes
- ☐ Scissors
- ☐ Markers
- ☐ Paintbrush
- ☐ Paint
- ☐ Paper
- ☐ Glue

1. Gather different sized boxes, such as cereal boxes, popcorn boxes, and noodle boxes.

2. Cut the top flaps off of each box where it was opened.

3. Cut off the back of each box.

4. Flip each box upside down so the bottom of the box becomes the roof of the building.

5. Draw doors and windows, and cut them out.

6. Paint the boxes. Let the paint dry.

7. Using paper, draw details, such as signs, roof shingles, or house numbers. Cut them out and glue them on the buildings.

8. Put the buildings side by side to create a city. You can make yards, roads, and trees to add to your city.

CONTINUED →

THE IMPORTANCE OF CARING FOR OUR PLANET

Earth is the only home we have, so it is important to take care of it. Earth gives us the air and water we need to live. If we can reduce the amount of pollution that we put into our water, air, and land, then we can keep the animals, plants, and people healthy and safe. Recycle everything you can. Reuse items such as containers, boxes, and bags. Try to reduce the amount of water you use by turning off the sink when you are brushing your teeth, and reduce the electricity you use by turning off the lights when you leave a room.

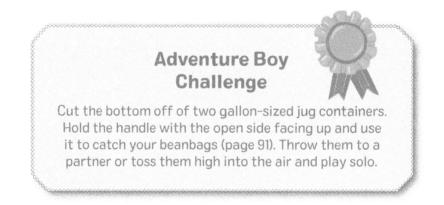

Adventure Boy Challenge

Cut the bottom off of two gallon-sized jug containers. Hold the handle with the open side facing up and use it to catch your beanbags (page 91). Throw them to a partner or toss them high into the air and play solo.

Clown Around

Adventure Boys can have fun and entertain people by learning and performing these cool tricks!

MAGIC TRICKS

With any magic trick, there are two important steps: preparation before the trick, and the story and movements you use during your trick.

The Ripped Paper Trick

Your friends will be amazed as you do this trick while blindfolded!

WHAT YOU'LL NEED

☐ Pen or pencil
☐ Paper
☐ Blindfold

1. Draw lines to divide a piece of paper into nine sections.

2. Give someone in the audience that piece of paper and a pen.

3. Ask them to write the name of an animal in the center square and write the names of food in all the other squares.

4. Have them tear (not cut) the paper on the lines into nine pieces and mix them up.

5. While blindfolded, you will feel each piece and find the only piece that has the animal written on it.

6. How will you know? As you are feeling the pieces, the middle piece is the only one that will have four rough sides from ripping. All the other pieces will have at least one straight side.

CONTINUED →

The Hidden Coin Trick

You and your assistant will leave your audience speechless with this special coin trick.

WHAT YOU'LL NEED

- ☐ Penny, nickel, dime, and quarter
- ☐ Table
- ☐ Coffee cup with a handle
- ☐ An assistant

1. Hand the four coins to an audience member and tell them that when you leave the room, they should pick one coin, set it on the table, and your assistant will cover it with a coffee cup. The audience member can hold on to the rest of the coins for safekeeping.

2. The trick here is that the assistant will set the cup down so the handle is pointing in a certain direction to give you a clue as to what coin is hiding under the cup.

   - If it is pointing toward 12 o'clock, the coin is a penny.

   - If it is pointing toward 3 o'clock, it is a nickel.

   - If it is pointing toward 6 o'clock, it will be a dime.

   - If it is pointing toward 9 o'clock, it will be a quarter.

Notice how the coins go from smallest to largest in value as the handle of the cup moves clockwise.

3. Come back into the room. Wave your hands around and say a few magic words to make it look like you are able to see through the cup or can sense the size of the coin underneath the cup.

4. Tell your audience which coin is under the cup and have your assistant lift the cup to reveal that you are right!

YO-YO TRICKS

The basic move of the yo-yo is to hold it in your hand with the loop around your middle finger. Flick your wrist, sending the yo-yo straight down. When it gets down to the bottom, give it a small tug upward and the yo-yo will come back to your hand. Practice this trick until it becomes easy. Then, give these more advanced tricks a try.

The Sleeper

1. Hold the yo-yo in your hand with your palm facing up.

2. Flick your wrist and send the yo-yo straight toward the ground. The yo-yo will stay spinning at the bottom.

3. While the yo-yo is spinning at the bottom, flip your palm over so it faces the ground.

4. Give the yo-yo a small tug upward, and it will return to your hand.

5. This is an important trick to practice over and over, because it is a step in many other yo-yo tricks.

> **Keep in Mind:** If your yo-yo spins and doesn't come back up, or if it comes right back up without spinning, try rewinding the string around the yo-yo clockwise.

Forward Pass

1. Hold the yo-yo in your hand with your arm down at your side. The yo-yo will be facing behind you and the back of your hand facing forward.

2. Swing your arm forward and throw the yo-yo out in front of you.

3. When the yo-yo reaches the end of the string, flip your hand over so your palm is facing up. Give the string a small tug and catch the yo-yo when it comes back to you.

Adventure Boy Challenge

Host a night of magic and yo-yo tricks for your friends and family. Practice your tricks before your performance and wow the audience with your new skills.

Imaginary Worlds

Have you ever wanted to travel to a faraway place, such as Antarctica or a magical kingdom? With a few friends, costumes, and your imagination, you can!

ROLE PLAYING

Live-action role playing, or LARPing, is a game with a group of people who pretend they are characters in a different world. It is a game of magic, slow-motion battles, and adventure.

Pirate Island

You can create any adventure for you and your friends to be a part of, but here is one to get you started:

1. Welcome to Pirate Island! Dress up in pirate gear. Use what you have for costumes or make your own.

2. Split up into two groups. Give each pirate crew a name and find something to be your ship (a hill, large rock, or group of bushes).

3. The crews can compete against each other by completing three missions to earn treasure. For each mission you can win three pieces of gold.

CONTINUED →

- Run a race
- Sword throwing contest (Who can throw a ball or stick the farthest?)
- Arm wrestling tournament
- Collect the most of something in 2 minutes (rocks, acorns, or sticks)
- Make up your own missions

4. Uh-oh! A sea monster is trying to sink your ships! Both crews should work together to fight it off to keep their gold.

5. The crew that wins the most gold is the best pirate crew in the land!

Adventure Boy Challenge

On Pirate Island, water bottles can be made into cannons, telescopes, or pirate hooks. Use cardboard to make hats, a treasure box, or swords.

A Green Thumb

Learning to grow and care for
Earth's plants is an important skill
for every Adventure Boy. Grow your
own food and care for plants that
attract and help different insects
and animals.

THE BASICS

Plants need sun, water, and soil to grow. However, each type of plant needs a different amount of each to thrive.

Sun

Some plants always need sun, some need just a few hours, while others prefer shade. Check the seed packet or do research to find how much sun your plant needs.

Water

Some plants require more water than others. If the soil feels dry when you poke it, give it more water. If water drains from your pot or the soil isn't soaking up the water anymore, it has enough water. Pour the water in the soil near the stem, not on the leaves. The roots are what need to be watered.

Soil

The best mixture of soil for growing a garden of herbs or vegetables is equal amounts of topsoil and compost. Try an even mixture of topsoil and coffee grounds, or buy it already mixed at a garden store.

Containers

Whether you are planting in large or small pots and containers, have holes in the bottom to allow for the water to drain. Take care of plants in containers the same way you would take care of plants in the ground.

GET GROWING

Here's how to plant and sprout seeds that can eventually be planted in a garden or container.

WHAT YOU'LL NEED

- ☐ Scissors
- ☐ Cardboard egg carton
- ☐ Pie pan or plate
- ☐ Soil
- ☐ Coffee grounds (optional)
- ☐ Seeds
- ☐ Water

1. Cut the sections of a cardboard egg carton apart. Set the sections in a pie pan or plate.

2. Fill each section more than halfway with soil. You can get soil from a garden store, or mix equal parts topsoil and coffee grounds.

3. Plant one or two seeds in each section by pushing the seed down and gently covering it with soil. Follow the instructions on the seed packet.

4. Keep a small amount of water in the pie pan or on the plate, and just the right amount of water will be absorbed into the soil from the bottom.

5. Once each seed has sprouted and grown two or three leaves, they are ready to plant in a garden or pot. You can keep them in the egg carton sections when you plant them. The cardboard will help keep the roots moist, and it is biodegradable.

6. If you are looking for seeds that sprout quickly, try lettuce, radishes, beans, or squash.

Adventure Boy Challenge

Did you know that you can use scraps of vegetables to regrow new ones? Put the end of a bunch of celery, head of lettuce, or stems of cilantro in a cup with the bottom of the vegetables in a small amount of water, and watch it grow. Once it has sprouted, plant it in a pot or your garden.

Cracking the Code

Codes are a different way to communicate with people and computers. Try these coding activities and then come up with your own.

FOLLOW THE SEQUENCE

Train your brain to think like a computer programmer by being very specific when explaining how to do something.

1. Think about each step that it takes to make a sandwich. Write down the steps for someone else to follow.

2. Be very specific about each step. For example, instead of saying "Get bread," you should say, "Get two pieces of bread out of the bag. Set them on a plate. Close the bag."

3. Have someone else read your directions about how to make a sandwich and ask them to do **exactly** what you have written. Did they make the sandwich like you wanted them to?

4. You can also write directions for how to brush your teeth, make a bed, or feed your pet.

WRITE IN BINARY

A computer uses binary code to store information. It is seven digits that only include 0s and 1s in different combinations. Zero (0) means electricity is off and 1 means electricity is on. Computer programmers, web developers, and software engineers use binary code.

Look at the chart and write your name using binary code. If your name is Jack, you would write:

1001010 1000001 1000011 1001011

Write a message to your friend and have them use the chart to decode it.

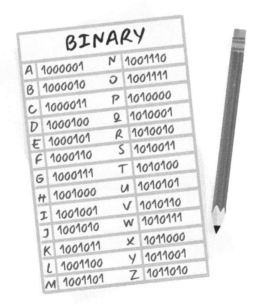

CODE A LEGO MAZE

You can make a Lego character or toy move through a maze by making a code for it to follow. If you can get the hang of coding with Legos, you can use your skills for other more difficult coding projects.

WHAT YOU'LL NEED

- ☐ Legos in assorted sizes
- ☐ Lego character or small toy
- ☐ Pencil
- ☐ Paper
- ☐ Scissors
- ☐ Tape

Level 1

Make a path with Legos by lining them up to look like a road. Have your path turn in different directions.

There are four choices, or commands, that you can use to get your character to move to the end of your path:

1. Go forward

2. Turn right

3. Turn left

4. End

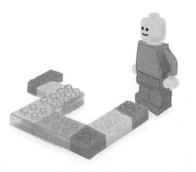

Each Lego brick (no matter the size) equals one command. Write down a command for each brick until your character gets to the end of the path. It might look something like this:

CONTINUED →

CODE A LEGO MAZE CONTINUED

1. Go forward
2. Go forward
3. Go forward
4. Turn right
5. Go forward
6. Go forward
7. Turn left
8. Go forward
9. Go forward
10. Go forward
11. End

Level 2

Cut a piece of paper into 1-inch squares and make a path with the squares by taping them together. Turn your path into a maze by having it split and go right AND left. One of those paths can end in a dead end, while the other will continue winding its way to the end.

Use your Legos to build walls around the path of your maze. Get creative by using tall walls and short walls, dead ends, and decorations.

Instead of repeating the same commands several times, shorten your code by writing it this way:

1. For 3 steps, go forward
2. End
3. Turn right
4. For 2 steps, go forward
5. End
6. Turn left
7. For 3 steps, go forward
8. End

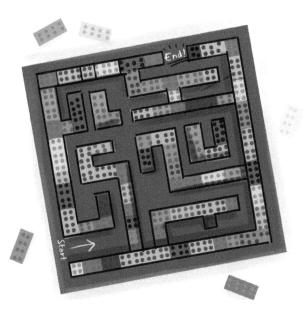

WHY CODE?

Coding is how we talk to computers. It is used to make websites, apps, and games. Coding teaches you how to plan out your thoughts and organize the way you share them. Use coding to make up a game for your friends, or use it to create something that helps the world!

Adventure Boy Challenge

Make an obstacle course and write a code for it. Have a friend or sibling follow the code you wrote to get themselves to the end of the course.

Social Sketch

Drawing is a great way Adventure Boys can express their ideas and show their creativity. From abstract sketches and geometric designs to people and characters, you can have hours of fun drawing by yourself or with friends.

CREATURE MASH-UP

Creature Mash-up is a creative drawing game that will have you and your friends laughing and drawing together.

WHAT YOU'LL NEED

- ☐ Scissors (optional)
- ☐ Paper
- ☐ Pencil
- ☐ Timer

1. Tear or cut a piece of paper in half lengthwise and fold it into three equal sections to make three squares.

2. The first person has 2 minutes to draw the head and neck of the creature on the top section of the paper. If you aren't sure what to draw, start with a shape like an oval, a square, or a triangle.

3. After 2 minutes, fold the top section of the paper backward so the second person cannot see what has been drawn, and pass it to them.

CONTINUED

4. The second person has 2 minutes to draw the body on the middle section of the paper. After 2 minutes of drawing, fold that section backward so the next person cannot see it, and pass it to them. The third person has 2 minutes to draw the bottom of the creature. It can be legs, a tail, or something unique.

5. Open up the paper and see the creature that you and your friends have created. You may need to add a few lines to connect the three parts.

Adventure Boy Challenge

Write a story about your favorite creature mash-up or make it into a sculpture out of clay.

Practice Kindness

Kindness can change the world!
By showing kindness to others
every day, you can make a big
difference.

MAKE A NEW FRIEND

Practice kindness by saying hello to or smiling at someone new. Look for someone who is sitting alone and ask to join them. If you are playing a game and there is someone who is left out, include them. When you see someone who looks like they are having a hard time, ask how you can help.

VOLUNTEER

Volunteering your time and energy to help your community is another way to practice kindness. There are many people who need help.

Create and keep "kindness" bags in your family's car filled with food, water, socks, or blankets. Then, you will be prepared to hand them out when you see someone that needs help.

You can spread joy by spending your time helping at a church, at a school, or in your city. Ask a local organization how you can start volunteering.

Adventure Boy Challenge

Small acts of kindness make a big difference! Hold a door for someone, cook for a neighbor, or help a family member. Set a goal of three acts of kindness per day.

Because You Deserve a Treat

After a fun day of hard work, it is nice to treat yourself to something special. Make your own ice cream and reward yourself with a sweet treat.

HOMEMADE ICE CREAM IN A BAG

Use chemistry to make your own ice cream! The ice and salt mixture pull the heat away from your ingredients so it can freeze into ice cream. Experiment with different amounts and types of salt each time you make ice cream.

WHAT YOU'LL NEED

- [ ] 2 zip-top bags, 1 quart-size and 1 gallon-size
- [ ] 1 cup half-and-half
- [ ] 2 tablespoons sugar
- [ ] 1 teaspoon vanilla extract
- [ ] Ice
- [ ] ¼ cup salt
- [ ] Dish towel
- [ ] Timer

1. In the quart-size zip-top bag, add the half-and-half, sugar, and vanilla extract. Seal the bag, pushing out any extra air.

2. Fill the gallon-size bag halfway with ice, and add the salt.

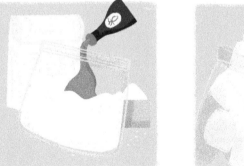 

CONTINUED →

3. Put the quart-size bag inside the gallon-size bag, on top of the ice, and add more ice. Seal the gallon-size bag.

4. Cover the bag with a towel or hold on to it with oven mitts, because it will get cold. Set a timer for 8 minutes and shake the bag until the ice cream freezes.

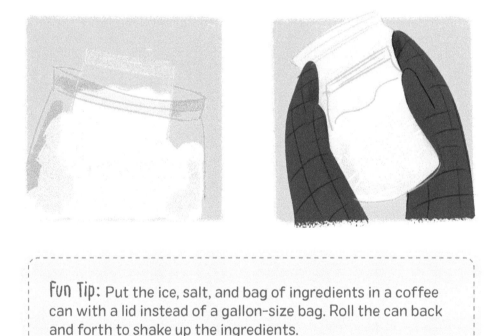

Fun Tip: Put the ice, salt, and bag of ingredients in a coffee can with a lid instead of a gallon-size bag. Roll the can back and forth to shake up the ingredients.

5. Take the bag of ice cream out of the gallon-size bag. Rinse it in cold water to get the salt off.

6. Open the bag, stir, and eat.

Adventure Boy Challenge

Host an ice-cream party for your friends! Have everyone make their own ice cream and offer different toppings to complete their treat.

10 ADVENTUROUS PEOPLE THROUGH HISTORY

Ibn al-Haytham (965–1040)
Ibn al-Haytham was a scientist and astronomer who invented the camera obscura (pinhole camera). He was the first to discover and explain concepts about how the eyes and the brain work together to see things.

Philip Emeagwali (1954–present)
Philip Emeagwali is called one of the "Fathers of the Internet." He figured out how one supercomputer could talk to six others at the same time. This made it possible for different computers to communicate quickly all over the world.

Lizzie Armanto (1993–present)
Lizzie Armanto is the first female skateboarder to complete the 360-degree vertical loop, which only a few skaters have been able to conquer. She is training to enter the 2021 Olympic Games.

Ruth Bader Ginsburg (1933–2020)
Ruth Bader Ginsburg was the second woman to serve on the United States Supreme Court. She stood up for others, even in difficult situations, so that everyone would have equal rights, especially women and minorities.

Jane Goodall (1934–present)

Jane Goodall became an expert on chimpanzees after studying them for 60 years in Tanzania. She fights to protect animals and the environment.

Ynes Mexia (1870–1938)

Ynes Mexia is a botanist who traveled to Mexico, South America, and Alaska, collecting 145,000 plant samples. She discovered 500 new plant species.

Matthew Henson (1866–1955)

Matthew Henson was one of the first African American explorers. Known for his explorations into the Arctic, he and his partner Robert Peary discovered the North Pole in 1909.

Ellen Ochoa (1958–present)

Ellen Ochoa was the first Hispanic woman to go to space. On her first trip, her crew studied the ozone layer that protects Earth. She became the director of NASA's Johnson Space Center in Texas.

Edme Hippolyte Marié-Davy (1820–1893)

Edme Marié-Davy was an inventor from France. He invented the periscope that was used in submarines during World War I to watch out for the enemy.

Georg Wilhelm Steller (1709–1746)

Georg Wilhelm Steller was a German naturalist who ended up in Alaska while looking for North America. Steller's jay and the Steller sea lion are named after him.

ABOUT THE AUTHOR

Nicole Duggan is the author of *Adventure Girls!* and a passionate educator with a master's degree and many years of experience in early childhood education. She is the founder of the blog The Activity Mom, where she inspires children to explore and create while empowering parents to connect with their children through learning.

ABOUT THE ILLUSTRATOR

Cait Brennan specializes in creating inspiring travel, nature, and adventure illustrations for kids and kids at heart. She works on all kinds of different projects, but especially loves books and has illustrated plenty of them since graduating with a BFA many years ago. In addition to drawing a lot, she also makes big messes in the kitchen and spends too much time chasing after her crazy dog. Take a peek at more of Cait's work at CaitBrennan.com.